The Ultimate Myrtle Beach Travel Guide

How to Make the Most of Your Trip to the Grand Strand

Alex Harper

Contents

1
Introduction

The Ultimate Myrtle Beach Travel Guide will tell you everything you need to know to make the most of your trip to the coast. From where to stay and what to eat, to the best activities. We've got you covered!

Myrtle Beach is a coastal city in South Carolina that's known for its beaches, golf courses, and attractions. The area was first settled by the English in 1684 but didn't become a popular tourist destination until the late 19th century, when wealthy Northerners began coming to the area to escape the cold winters.

Today, Myrtle Beach is one of the most popular vacation spots on the East Coast, with millions of visitors each year. The city is home to many large hotels and resorts, as well as countless restaurants, shops, and entertainment options. There's something for everyone in Myrtle Beach, making it the perfect place to enjoy a fun-filled vacation with family and friends.

The area provides a large variety of choices for dining, entertainment, adventures, annual events, and romance. I will provide you with the best of these choices later on in this book. Myrtle beach is truly a magical place to visit!

The temperatures average around 86 °F during the summer with high humidity. The weather can change with little to no warning from a sunny day to a rain shower, then back again. We often joke that if you don't like the weather... just wait five minutes and it will change.

The winters are short and mild and rarely go below 32° F. Even during the coldest months, all you really need is a hooded sweatshirt or a light jacket to be comfortable.

So pack your sunscreen and your sense of adventure, and get ready for a beach vacation you'll never forget.

10 Must-Have Items For Your Beach Vacation

1. **Waterproof Camera:** Want to take pictures of you and your family on the beach? This is the camera to get. It will protect your camera from water damage. You can also use this camera for underwater photography. It's a great way to remember your trip. I prefer a waterproof phone case over a separate camera because it has everything in one place, but that's just me.

2. **Beach Blanket:** I love this kind of blanket because it's big enough for the whole family. It's a great item to have if you plan on spending time at the beach or pool. You can easily fold it up and stick it in your bag when not in use.

3. **Beach Ball:** These are so much fun for kids! They like to chase them around and throw them in the air. You can also play games with your kids using these beach balls.

4. **Beach Umbrella:** It's great to have a beach umbrella if you plan on spending a lot of time at the beach. It will give you shade and protect your skin from the sun. I personally like to use this beach umbrella when I'm tanning because it gives me a nice opaque shade.

5. **Beach Towels:** These are great for keeping the sun off of your skin and also protecting you from the sand. They are also easy to carry around if you plan on going to multiple beaches.

6. **Beach Toys:** They will keep your kids busy and entertained all day. My favorite toys are sand molds. They make it fun to sculpt with the sand and we can even use them as a scoop for collecting shells.

7. **Bathing Suits:** Bathing suits are always a must-have for the summer. I personally like to get a few different ones. You never know when you will want to change it up from your normal suit.

8. **Flip Flops:** They are great to throw on when you go to the bathroom or want to walk around the hotel.

9. **Water Bottle:** I always make sure that I have a water bottle when we go away. It is easy to get dehydrated when you are out in the sun all day.

10. **Sunscreen:** We all know how important sunscreen is in the summer. I bring a few different types with me.

3

Top 10 Places to Stay

1. **The Breakers Resort:** The Breakers offers an array of activities and amenities for its guests. From its heated indoor and outdoor pools to its lazy river and water slides, there is something for everyone at The Breakers.

Besides its many recreational options, The Breakers also boasts a variety of dining choices. Guests can enjoy anything from a casual poolside lunch to an elegant dinner at one of the resort's five restaurants. And with a convenient location just steps from the beach, it's easy to see why The Breakers is such a popular choice for vacationers.

2. **Marriott's OceanWatch Villas:** Marriott's OceanWatch Villas offers stunning ocean views, spacious villas, and top-notch amenities. From the moment you arrive, you'll feel like royalty. The valet will take your car and they will bring your bags to your room. You can relax by the pool, get a massage at the spa, or play golf at one of the many nearby courses. Marriott's OceanWatch Villas offer all the comforts of home with the added luxury of a beachfront resort. The two- and three-bedroom villas have fully equipped kitchens, separate living and dining areas, and private balconies with ocean views. Guests at Marriott's OceanWatch Villas can enjoy access to an outdoor pool, a fitness center, and a restaurant.

3. **Kingston Plantation Condos:** Kingston Plantation is one of the most popular condo complexes in Myrtle Beach. This 145-acre oceanfront resort features one-, two-, and three-bedroom units, as well as a variety of on-site amenities.

Visitors to Kingston Plantation will enjoy its spacious accommodations and array of first-class amenities, which include an oceanfront pool, lazy river, fitness center, and spa. The complex is also home to several restaurants, including the award-winning Logan's Roadhouse.

Whether you're looking for a relaxing getaway or an action-packed vacation, Kingston Plantation has something for everyone. So pack your bags and head to the coast for some fun in the sun!

4. **Sea Mist Resort:** Sea Mist Resort is a top vacation destination for families and couples alike. The resort features a wide range of activities and amenities, making it the perfect place to relax and unwind. Sea Mist Resort is just minutes from all the best attractions and activities the city offers. Families will love the on-site water park with its slides and pools, while couples can enjoy a romantic dinner at one of the resort's many restaurants. Regardless of what you're looking for on a vacation, Sea Mist Resort will have something for everyone.

5. **The Palms:** This oceanfront resort offers something for everyone, from luxurious accommodations to exciting on-site amenities. Here are some tips to help you make the most of your trip to The Palms.

Start your day with a delicious breakfast at one of The Palms' on-site restaurants. Then, head down to the beach for a day of sun and fun! Take a dip in the ocean, build sandcastles with the kids, or just relax on the shore and soak up the rays.

In the afternoon, explore all that The Palms offers. Take a swim in one of the resort's three pools, play a game of tennis or volleyball, or enjoy a refreshing drink at one of the bars.

6. **Crown Reef Beach Resort and Waterpark:** If you're looking for a Myrtle Beach resort that has it all, look no further than Crown Reef Resort. This beachfront property offers plenty of activities for guests of all ages, making it the perfect place to vacation with the whole family.

The resort features an on-site water park with slides and a lazy river, as well as a kids' club with daily activities. There's also a fitness center and spa for adults, plus plenty of shops and restaurants on-site. And of course, the beautiful beach is just steps away from your room.

7. **Captain's Quarters Resort:** The resort offers a variety of accommodations, from standard rooms to suites and villas. Guests can enjoy the on-site pool, fitness center, and spa, or venture out to explore the many shops and restaurants nearby. Whether you're looking for a relaxing vacation or an action-packed getaway, the Captain's Quarters Resort is the perfect place for you.

Captain's Quarters also has a wide variety of dining options, including a buffet and a casual restaurant. Guests can also enjoy the many shops and attractions that are located nearby.

8. Hilton Myrtle Beach Resort: The resort offers a wide range of amenities, including an outdoor pool, lazy river, fitness center, and spa. Guest rooms are spacious and well-appointed, with private balconies overlooking the ocean.

The resort is on the oceanfront and offers a variety of amenities, including an outdoor pool, a fitness center, and a spa. The rooms at the Hilton Myrtle Beach Resort are spacious and well-appointed, and the hotel staff are friendly and helpful.

If you're looking for a luxurious and relaxing vacation destination, Hilton Myrtle Beach Resort is the perfect place for you. With its beautiful location, top-notch amenities, and excellent service, you'll have everything you need to enjoy a fabulous beach vacation.

9. Dunes Village Resort: The accommodations at Dunes Village Resort are second to none. All the rooms and suites have private balconies with stunning views of the Atlantic Ocean. And inside the units, you'll find plenty of space and all the modern conveniences you need, including fully equipped kitchens.

When it comes to recreation, Dunes Village Resort has something for everyone. There are five outdoor pools, a lazy river, a water park with slides and a spray-ground, and a state-of-the-art fitness center.

10. Avista Resort: Whether you're looking to relax by the pool or take a stroll on the beach. Avista Resort is the perfect base camp. The resort's convenient location puts you just minutes away from all the best attractions, dining, and shopping that the Grand Strand offers.

Whether you're looking to hit the links on one of Myrtle Beach's famed golf courses, enjoy some time relaxing on the beach, or explore the area's many attractions, Avista Resort is the perfect place to stay. This oceanfront property offers one- and two-bedroom suites, each with a full kitchen and private balcony. Guests can take advantage of on-site amenities like an outdoor pool, fitness center, and game room, or venture out to nearby attractions like Broadway at the Beach and Ripley's Aquarium.

4

Top 10 Places to Eat

When you're planning a trip to Myrtle Beach, one of the first things you need to do is figure out where you're going to eat. With so many options, it's hard to narrow it down. Here are 10 of the best restaurants in Myrtle Beach that you definitely need to check out.

1. **Boardwalk Billy's Raw Bar and Grill:** This local favorite is known for its fresh seafood and its laid-back atmosphere. The restaurant is located right on the boardwalk, so you can enjoy the view of the ocean while you eat. Be sure to try one of their famous oyster shooters and wash it down with a cold beer. You'll feel like a true local after spending some time at Boardwalk Billy's.

2. **Croissants Bistro and Bakery:** Croissants Bistro and Bakery is a must-visit spot for anyone traveling to Myrtle Beach. The bakery offers a wide variety of freshly baked pastries, bread, and desserts, all of which are made with locally sourced ingredients. The bistro portion of the business serves breakfast, lunch, and dinner, with an emphasis on French fare. Whether you're looking for a quick snack or a leisurely meal, Croissants Bistro and Bakery is sure to please. Plus, their coffee is amazing!

3. **Carolina Roadhouse:** If you're looking for a great Myrtle Beach steakhouse, Carolina Roadhouse is the place to go. They cook the steaks to perfection and the service is top-notch. You'll definitely want to try their famous onion rings, too. Carolina Roadhouse is the perfect spot for a romantic dinner or a night out with friends. They serve Southern favorites, including fall-off-the-bone Baby Back Ribs, giant Seafood platters, and lump Crap Dip- served warm with old bay pretzels for a true southern experience.

4. The Melting Pot Restaurant of Myrtle Beach: For a truly unique dining experience, try out The Melting Pot. They offer an amazing fondue experience that you are unlikely to forget. With different fondues, from your main entrée all the way to your dessert.

5. Captain George's Seafood Restaurant: This local favorite offers an incredible variety of fresh seafood, from oysters and shrimp to crabs and lobster. The prices are very reasonable, and the quality of the food is outstanding.

If you're looking for a truly memorable dining experience while you're in Myrtle Beach, check out Captain George's Seafood Restaurant. You won't be disappointed!

6. Thoroughbreds Chophouse & Seafood Grille: The Thoroughbreds Chophouse & Seafood Grille is one of Myrtle Beach's most popular restaurants, and it's easy to see why. The menu features a wide variety of seafood and steak options, all of which are cooked to perfection. The atmosphere is casual yet classy, and the service is always top-notch. Whether you're in the mood for a romantic dinner for two or a night out with friends, you'll have a great time at the Thoroughbreds Chophouse & Seafood Grille.

7. Carolina Pancake House: Carolina Pancake House is a local favorite for breakfast and brunch. The restaurant has been serving up hot pancakes, waffles, and eggs since opening in Myrtle Beach in 2010. Carolina Pancake House is known for its friendly staff and home-style cooking. The menu features all the breakfast classics, including pancakes, waffles, eggs, bacon, sausage, omelets, and french toast. Carolina Pancake House also offers a variety of lunch options, including sandwiches, salads, and soup.

Whether you're looking for a quick bite before hitting the beach or a leisurely meal to start your day, Carolina Pancake House is the perfect spot. The restaurant is open daily from 6:00 am to 2:00 pm.

8. **Mr. Fish:** Mr. Fish is one of the best, serving up fresh catches from the Atlantic daily. The menu has something for everyone, whether you're in the mood for fried shrimp, grilled fish, or a lobster tail. And don't forget to try the hush puppies - they're some of the best you'll ever have!

9. **Angelo's Steak & Pasta:** Angelo's Steak & Pasta is a local favorite at Myrtle Beach. The family-friendly restaurant has been serving up mouth-watering dishes since 1978. The secret to their success is simple—they only use the freshest ingredients and cook each meal to perfection.

If you're looking for a delicious steak dinner, Angelo's is the place to go. They cook the steaks exactly how you like them and served with a variety of sides, including their famous garlic mashed potatoes. For something a little lighter, the shrimp scampi is a great option. They cook the pasta al dente and tossed in a light garlic butter sauce.

No matter what you order, you will enjoy your meal at Angelo's Steak & Pasta.
- If you enjoy Italian cuisine, you will love Angelo's. It features a buffet that includes all the lasagna, spaghetti, ravioli, meatballs, and pizza that you could want. They have everything from seafood to burgers!

10. **Punta Cana Dominican Grill:** If you're looking for a taste of the Dominican Republic while visiting Myrtle Beach, look no further than Punta Cana Dominican Grill. This restaurant offers traditional Dominican dishes like empanadas, tostones, and chicharrones, as well as more familiar fare like burgers and sandwiches. The portions are hearty, so you will leave with a full stomach. The atmosphere is casual and relaxed, making it a great spot for a family dinner or a night out with friends.

5

Top 10 Places to Go

1. **Broadway at the Beach:** This giant complex has something for everyone, from shops and restaurants to entertainment and nightlife. You could easily spend a whole day here exploring everything it offers.

If you're looking for shopping, Broadway at the Beach has you covered. There are plenty of stores to browse, whether you're looking for souvenirs or beachwear. If you get hungry, there are plenty of restaurants to choose from, including fast food options and more upscale dining. And when you're ready to relax or have some fun, there are bars, clubs, a movie theater, and even an aquarium.

No matter what your interests are, Broadway at the Beach is sure to have something for you.

2. **Hit the beach:** Visit the beach, of course! Myrtle Beach is known for its gorgeous beaches. Soak up the sun, go swimming, build sandcastles, or just relax on the shore.

3. **Take a drive to the town of Pawleys Island:** A small town in Georgetown County, South Carolina. The town is known for its laid-back atmosphere and its beautiful beaches. Visitors to Pawleys Island can enjoy fishing, kayaking, swimming, and sunbathing. The town is also home to several restaurants, shops, and art galleries.

4. **Visit the Market Commons:** This unique shopping center is on the site of what used to be a bustling produce market. The market closed in the 1960s, but they have brought it back to life as an upscale shopping destination.

5. **Ride the SkyWheel:** The SkyWheel is a 200-foot tall Ferris wheel that offers breathtaking views of the Myrtle Beach coastline. Not only is it one of the tallest Ferris wheels in North America, but it is also the only one with climate-controlled gondolas. This means that no matter what the weather is like outside, you can always enjoy a comfortable ride.

Each gondola can accommodate up to 6 people, so it's perfect for groups or families. The ride itself lasts about 10 minutes, giving you plenty of time to take in the scenery.

6. **Ripley's Aquarium of Myrtle Beach:** The aquarium has over 10,000 sea creatures, including sharks, stingrays, and sea turtles. Visitors can see the animals up close in over 350,000 gallons of water. The aquarium also has a 4D theater and a hands-on stingray touch pool.

Ripley's Aquarium is open 365 days a year and is located in Broadway at the Beach. Admission for adults (age 12+) is $36.99, children (ages 6-11) are $24.99, and children (ages 3-5) are $12.99. Seniors (age 65+) and military personnel get a discount with ID. There are also combo tickets available that include other Ripley's attractions in Myrtle Beach, such as the Believe It or Not! Odditorium or the Haunted Adventure.

7. **See a show at the House of Blues:** The House of Blues features a variety of musical acts, from local bands to nationally known artists. Visitors can enjoy a meal at the venue's restaurant before or after the show. The House of Blues is

in the heart of Myrtle Beach, making it easy to get to from anywhere in the city. The outdoor shows are also dog-friendly!

8. **Take a tour of Brookgreen Gardens:** Brookgreen Gardens is a must-see for any nature lover visiting Myrtle Beach. The gardens span 9,100 acres and are home to over 1,400 sculptures by American artists. Besides the beautiful sculptures, visitors can also enjoy the gardens' many flowers, birds, and other wildlife.

9 **Explore Myrtle Beach State Park:** Myrtle Beach State Park is one of the most popular tourist destinations in the United States. The park is in Myrtle Beach, South Carolina and is known for its beautiful beaches and its many attractions.

The park is open all year round and offers a variety of activities for visitors to enjoy. In the summer, the beach is a popular spot for swimming, sunbathing, and fishing. The state park also has a campground that is open to visitors who want to stay overnight. There are also several hiking trails that wind through the woods and offer views of the ocean.

10. **Visit the 14th Avenue Pier:** The 14th Avenue Pier is one of the most popular attractions in Myrtle Beach. Stretching over 1,000 feet into the Atlantic Ocean, the pier provides stunning views of the coastline. And is a great place to fish, sunbathe, or just take a leisurely stroll. There are also several restaurants

and cafes at the pier, making it the perfect spot to grab a bite while enjoying the beautiful ocean views.

The pier is more than a mile long and overlooks over 4 miles of shoreline.

If you have time, check out some of the many golf courses available as well. The area is home to over 100 golf courses, most of which are along sandy white beaches. The layout of Myrtle Beach is unique in that it's split into three sections: North End, South End, and the Strip. The North End is home to the area's best golf courses, while the South End focuses on family-friendly activities. The Strip is where you'll find all the area's hotels, casinos, and entertainment venues.

6

Top 10 Places to Shop

Myrtle Beach is a top destination for beach lovers and shoppers alike. Here are the 10 best places to shop at Myrtle Beach:

1. **Hammock Shops Village:** Hammock Shops Village is a unique shopping destination located in the heart of Myrtle Beach. This quaint village is home to a variety of specialty shops, boutiques, and restaurants. Visitors can enjoy a leisurely stroll through the village while browsing the unique selection of merchandise. Hammock Shops Village is the perfect place to find that special something for yourself or a loved one.

2. **The Market Common:** The Market Common is one of the best places to stay while in town. This open-air shopping center and residential area is near the beach and has everything you need for a fun and relaxing trip.

The Market Common has something for everyone, with its mix of shops, restaurants, and entertainment options. You can find everything from stylish boutiques to beach gear, and there are plenty of dining choices to suit any taste. After a day of exploring or relaxing on the beach, head to The Market Common for some evening entertainment. There are several bars and clubs here that offer live music or dancing, so you can keep the party going all night long.

3. **Coastal Grand Mall:** Coastal Grand Mall is the largest shopping mall in Myrtle Beach. It is located just off of Highway 501 and contains Belk, JC Penney, Dick's Sporting Goods, and Bass Pro Shops. The mall features over 150 stores and restaurants, making it the perfect place to find everything you need for your Myrtle Beach vacation.

Whether you're looking for beachwear, souvenirs, or simply a place to relax and escape the heat, Coastal Grand Mall is the perfect spot. Be sure to check out the food court for a quick bite or sit down meal and don't forget to pick up a seashell or two from one of the many gift shops.

4. **Eagles Beachwear:** Eagles Beachwear is a must-stop shop for anyone visiting the Myrtle Beach area. The store offers a wide variety of beachwear, including swimsuits, coverups, and accessories, all at affordable prices. Eagles Beachwear also has a helpful staff that can assist you in finding the perfect outfit for your beach day.

5. **Tanger Outlets:** Tanger Outlets is one of the best places to shop in Myrtle Beach. With over 100 stores, you're sure to find what you're looking for. And if you're looking for a bargain, Tanger Outlets is the place to be. You can find great deals on name-brand clothing, shoes, and more.

If you're visiting Myrtle Beach during the summer, be sure to stop by Tanger Outlets. You'll find everything you need to stay cool, including sunglasses, swimwear, and sandals. And if you're looking for souvenirs to take home, Tanger Outlets has a great selection of beach-themed items.

No matter what time of year you visit Myrtle Beach, Tanger Outlets is always a great place to shop.

6. **Gay Dolphin Gift Cove:** Gay Dolphin Gift Cove has been a fixture on the Myrtle Beach Boardwalk for over 60 years. The store is known for its wide selection of souvenirs, beachwear, and unique gifts. But what really sets Gay Dolphin apart is its friendly staff and relaxed atmosphere.

Whether you're looking for the perfect souvenir to remember your trip to Myrtle Beach or just want to browse the wide selection of items, Gay Dolphin Gift Cove is definitely worth a visit.

7. **Everything Under the Sun Flea Market:** There's no better place to find souvenirs and coastal-inspired home decor than at the Everything Under the Sun Flea Market. With over 400 vendor booths, this market has something for everyone. You'll find everything from handcrafted jewelry and art to vintage finds and new home decor.

Whether you're looking for a unique gift for a friend or a special piece to add to your own collection, you will find it at the Everything Under the Sun Flea Market. Be sure to bargain with the vendors for the best deals on your purchases!

8. **Broadway at the Beach:** Broadway at the Beach is a large outdoor shopping, dining, and entertainment complex that features over 100 stores and restaurants, plus attractions like an aquarium, a zip line, and a Ferris wheel. Visitors can easily spend a whole day here exploring everything that Broadway at the Beach offers. Whether you're looking for souvenirs, beach gear, or just want to grab a bite to eat, you'll find it all here.

9. **Barefoot Landing:** Barefoot Landing is one of the most popular tourist destinations in Myrtle Beach. The area is home to many shops, restaurants, and attractions. Visitors can find everything from beachwear to souvenirs at the many shops in Barefoot Landing. There are also a variety of restaurants, ranging from fast food to fine dining. Barefoot Landing also has a number of attractions, such as Aligator Adventure, Alabama Theatre, and Crooked Hammock Brewery Tours. With so much to do, Barefoot Landing is a great place to visit for a day or a week.

10. **Europa Market:** Europa Market is one of the best places to start your Myrtle Beach adventure. This open-air market is full of local vendors selling everything from handmade jewelry to fresh produce. You'll definitely want to take some time to explore all that Europa Market offers.

After you've had your fill of shopping, head on over to the nearby Myrtle Beach State Park. This park is a great place to relax and take in the natural beauty of the area. There are also plenty of activities available, including hiking, biking, and fishing.

7

Top 10 Nightlife Activities

1. **The Bowery:** The Bowery is a historic district in Myrtle Beach, South Carolina. The area is known for its nightlife, with bars, clubs, and restaurants lining

the streets. Visitors can also find shops and galleries in the area. The Bowery is a popular destination for tourists and locals alike.

2. **3001 Nightlife:** Myrtle Beach is home to some of the best nightlife on the East Coast, and the 3001 Club is one of the hottest spots. This club is known for its amazing light show, which features over 300 lights that change color and patterns in sync with the music. The club also has two dance floors, a VIP section, and a state-of-the-art sound system, which makes it the perfect place to party all night long. If you're looking for a place to let loose and have a great time, the 3001 Club is definitely the place for you.

3. **Spanish Galleon Night Club:** One of the best places to experience the nightlife is at the Spanish Galleon Night Club. They styled this club after a pirate ship and offers live entertainment nightly. Visitors can enjoy dancing, drinks, and plenty of fun!

Spanish Galleon Night Club is one of the most popular nightspots in Myrtle Beach. Themed after a pirate ship, the club offers live entertainment every night. Visitors can enjoy dancing, drinks, and having a great time! The club also has a restaurant that serves up delicious seafood dishes. Whether you're looking to dance the night away or enjoy a meal with friends, Spanish Galleon Night Club is the place to be!

4. **Comedy Cabana:** Comedy Cabana has been entertaining tourists and locals alike for over 26 years and features some of the best comedians in the country. The club is just a short walk from the beach. It's also close to many other attractions, making it easy to make a night of it.

If you're looking for a good laugh while on vacation, be sure to check out Comedy Cabana.

5. **Fat Harold's Beach Club:** If you're looking for a fun, lively beach club to enjoy during your Myrtle Beach vacation, look no further than Fat Harold's Beach Club. This popular club has been a Myrtle Beach staple since the 1950s, and it's easy to see why. From the moment you step inside, the friendly staff and the vibrant atmosphere 'll greet you. The dance floor is always packed with people of all ages enjoying live music and dancing the night away. There's also a full bar where you can enjoy refreshing cocktails while taking in the stunning ocean views. Whether you're looking to dance the night away or simply relax with a drink in hand, Fat Harold's Beach Club is the perfect spot to do it.

6. **OD Arcade & Lounge:** If you want to enjoy a bit of everything that Myrtle Beach offers, then the OD Arcade & Lounge is the perfect spot for you. This family-friendly establishment has something for everyone, whether you want to play some games, enjoy some delicious food, or just relax with a drink in hand.

The arcade features classic games like Pac-Man and Donkey Kong, as well as newer favorites like Mario Kart and Call of Duty. And if you get hungry while you're gaming, the lounge offers a menu of American comfort food staples like burgers, fries, and wings. There's also a full bar if you need to quench your thirst.

So whether you're looking for a place to have some fun or just want to take a break from the sun and sand, be sure to check out the OD Arcade & Lounge during your next trip to Myrtle Beach.

7. **Ocean Annie's:** Annie's Oceanfront Bar & Grill is a local favorite in Myrtle Beach. With its convenient location on the boardwalk and its delicious seafood, it's no wonder why! The menu features fresh, local seafood and burgers, sandwiches, and salads. And don't forget to try one of their famous cocktails! Whether you're looking for a light lunch or a late-night snack, Annie's is the place to go.

8. **Dead Dog Saloon:** If you're looking for a fun and unique Myrtle Beach experience, look no further than the Dead Dog Saloon. This casual eatery is located right on the water and offers a great view of the ocean. The menu features all your favorite American comfort foods, plus some local specialties like shrimp and grits. And of course, no visit to the Dead Dog Saloon would be complete without trying one of their signature cocktails. The bartenders are always happy to make something special just for you. So whether you're stopping in for a quick bite or staying all day to enjoy the views, the Dead Dog Saloon will make your Myrtle Beach trip one to remember.

9. **Riptydz:** Riptydz is one of the best places to eat at Myrtle Beach. The menu has something for everyone, and the food is always fresh and delicious. Plus, the view of the ocean from Riptydz is unbeatable. If you're looking for a place to watch the sunset, this is it.

Riptydz is also a great place to catch some live music. Local and regional bands play here often, and it's always a good time. Riptydz is a great place to relax, have some fun and enjoy the Carolina beach life.

10. **Señor Frog:** If you're looking for a party while you're in Myrtle Beach, look no further than Señor Frog. This bar and restaurant are known for its festive atmosphere and delicious drinks. The menu features Mexican favorites like tacos and quesadillas, as well as American classics like burgers and fries. There's also a full bar, so you can order your favorite cocktail or beer. And if you're feeling really adventurous, try the Frog Shot, a mix of vodka, rum, tequila, and grenadine. Señor Frog is open late, so it's the perfect place to go for a night out on the town.

8
Conclusion

When you're planning a trip to Myrtle Beach, there are a few things you should keep in mind to make the most of your vacation. First, think about what kind of activities you and your family or friends want to do while you're here. There's plenty to choose from, whether you want to hit the beach, golf, shop, or take in some local attractions. Whether you are looking to relax on the beach, get active outdoors, or enjoy the nightlife, Myrtle Beach has something for everyone. Myrtle Beach is more than just a beach town. It s a year-round destination with something for everyone. So pack your bags and head to Myrtle Beach for an unforgettable vacation. And last but not least, don't forget to pack your sunscreen!

If you found this book helpful, I'd be very appreciative if you left a favorable review for the book on Amazon!